THE HAWAIIAN Lei

A Tradition of Aloha

Bishop Museum

Mahalo Nui Loa

to the following individuals
who opened their homes and hearts to assist us:

The Bishop Museum gift shop

Fred and May Funakura

Ralph and Jessie Hashimoto

Laurie and Richard Hiramoto

Donald and Florence Izumi

Loretta Le and Wenda Fujiwara
Lin's Lei Shop

Maile Lee
Maile's Lei Stand

Mr. and Mrs. Wilfred Toki

Glenn Vea

Bessie Watson
Bessie's Lei Stand

Judy and Henry Wong

Tom and Jane Yamane

Ellarene Yasuhara
Irene's Lei Stand

THE HAWAIIAN *Lei*

A Tradition of Aloha

Ronn Ronck

Photographer Ray Wong

Lei Consultant Robz Yamane

ALAKA`I FLORAL CREATIONS, INC.

MUTUAL PUBLISHING

Library of Congress Catalog Card
Number: 97-73682

First Printing, November 1997

Design by Jane Hopkins

1 2 3 4 5 6 7 8 9

Softcover
ISBN 1-56647-169-9

Casebound
ISBN 1-56647-194-X

Mutual Publishing
1215 Center Street, Suite 210
Honolulu, Hawaii 96816
Telephone (808) 732-1709
Fax (808) 734-4094
e-mail: mutual@lava.net

Printed in Taiwan

Table of Contents

May Day in Hawai'i is a time to celebrate the craftsmanship and artistry of our island *lei* makers. On this, the first day of May, our children learn *lei* weaving, vendors offer up floral *lei* in parks and make-shift stands, and young and old proudly display their *haku, wili*, and shell *lei*.

Hawai'i, Land of *Lei*

Everybody wears *lei* in Hawai'i. They are a symbol of *aloha*, a token of greeting and a sign of friendship and love. You'll see them at parties, dances, graduations, weddings, and at the airport. Their rainbow colors and exotic fragrances delight the senses, open our hearts, and remind us that the smell of a pretty flower is still one of life's great pleasures.

Airport *lei* vendors display their *lei* in colorful floral arrangements of vanda orchid, tuberose, plumeria, *ti* leaf, carnation, *pua kenikeni*, and crown flower.

Hawai'i's beautiful *lei* are worn for special occasions but in Hawai'i any occasion can be special. An island birthday or anniversary just wouldn't be the same without sunbursts of *'ilima*, the perfumed scents of ginger and plumeria, and the spicy twists of *maile*. While some ancient Hawaiian practices have faded from sight, the art of *lei* making has managed to survive and thrive.

When Isabella Bird visited Hawai'i in 1873, she found herself surrounded by a sea of flowers. "Without an exception," she wrote, "the men and women wore wreaths and garlands of flowers, carmine, orange, or pure white, twined around their hats, and thrown carelessly around their necks, flowers unknown to me, but redolent of the tropics in fragrance and color."

The giving and wearing of neck and head *lei* can be traced back to the earliest human beings. Archeologists have found the remains of primitive bone, teeth, and shell necklaces scattered throughout the world. It is likely that the first forest dwellers also adorned themselves with a variety of leaves, flowers, and feathers.

Here in the Pacific, *lei* customs spread from Asia to the various Polynesian islands and reached their greatest expression in Hawai'i. Certain *lei* and garlands became associated with chiefly rank, the *hula* and other religious ceremonies, extended families, and geographical locations. The most skilled *lei* makers were honored members of their community, celebrated for their ability to adorn the body with nature's beauty.

Captain James Cook's arrival in 1778, and the introduction of Western culture and religion threw Hawaiian society into turmoil. Traditional *lei* making went into a decline as the *hula* was discouraged and the old ways of doing things became less important. *Lei* flowers were devastated by new insect pests and the indigenous birds once harvested for feather capes and *lei* vanished from the cleared forests.

Hawaiian traditions made an official comeback when King Kalakaua took the throne in 1874. The "Merrie Monarch" threw lavish *luau*, brought back the *hula*, and had gorgeous flower *lei* placed around the necks of his guests. During his reign Hawaiian men and women wore *lei* as part of their everyday attire.

Today the *lei* tradition is as strong as ever. It doesn't matter if you're proud to be a *kamaaina* (longtime resident) or happy to be a *malihini* (newcomer). Make a *lei*, give a *lei*, wear a *lei*. It's beautiful to be in Hawai'i.

Shell Seekers

Niihau residents gather the sea shells for their *lei* during the stormy winter months when the high surf wash large deposits of shells onto the sandy beaches. Shells are taken home, dried, and sorted according to type, color, and size. Experienced *lei* makers stock up on shells during the winter and practice their craft during the summer when less shells are available.

Lei of Old

Hawai'i was first settled more than a thousand years ago by brown-skinned Polynesian seafarers who ventured forth from the Marquesas and Society Islands. They brought their rich culture with them, including the ancient traditions of chant, dance, and *lei*-making. In their new home they found an abundance of natural *lei* materials along the warm, sandy shores and flower-filled forests.

Shell and seed *lei* and hat bands of multicultural origin grace the sellers' tables at a May Day *lei* celebration.

The grandest *lei* worn by the Hawaiians was the *lei niho palaoa*. It featured a hook-shaped pendant carved from a sperm whale's tooth that was hung around the neck on strands of tightly-braided human hair. This permanent *lei*, a symbol of chiefly rank, can be seen in the portrait drawings and watercolors made by the first Western artists who visited Hawai'i.

When Captain Cook visited Hawai'i he reported that some of the islanders wore strands of *kukui* or candlenuts. Mature nuts of the *kukui* were gathered after they fell from the tree, punctured, cleaned out, and strung through the center. They were polished to a beautiful blond, deep-brown, or black. Smaller seeds such as the red *wiliwili* and the black *manele* were also strung into *lei*. *Kukui* nut and various seed *lei* can now be found in gift shops throughout the Islands.

Shells have long been an important part of Hawaiian culture. The trumpets that announced the arrival of Captain Cook were made of large triton and helmet shells that had their spine tips filed off to make a blowhole. Fish hooks, food scrapers, and children's toys were made from other available shells.

Lei were also made from sea shells. The early European explorers recorded seeing numerous examples of shell *lei* in Hawai'i and some of these are now in museum collections. Shell *lei* were made on every island but the most highly prized shell *lei*, both then and now, are strung with small white, brown, and reddish shells washed by the ocean's waves onto the beaches of Niihau.

During the Victorian age, lustrous shell *lei* were nearly as coveted as pearls with Hawai'i's royal ladies. Queen Kapiolani, Queen Emma, and other high-born women wore long dresses and multiple loops of treasured Niihau shell *lei*. During the late 19th and early 20th-century, islanders also beaded strands of the tiny shells into long, swishing curtains to separate the rooms in their houses.

Shell *lei* and hat bands remain a popular fashion accessory in Hawai'i as well as in the islands of French Polynesia, Tonga, Fiji, and Samoa. Prices range from several dollars for those found at sidewalk souvenir stands to hundreds of dollars for true museum-quality Niihau shell *lei*. If you're going to spend big bucks, however, be sure to get some expert advice and deal with a reputable shop.

A Hawaiian woman wears a double strand *maile lei* and four strands of *pakalana* in this regal 1920s portrait. *Bishop Museum*

Bedecked in *lei* of greeting, Duke Kahanamoku, Richard Arlen, Douglas Fairbanks, Sr., and Clark Irvine pose at pier-side at Honolulu Harbor. ***Bishop Museum***

A vendor stands at Pier 6/7 on Boat Day and displays her exotic flower *lei* to the newly arrived visitors from the Matson steamer ship. ***Bishop Museum***

Legendary *Maile*

The ancient Greeks and Romans placed a wreath of green laurel on the heads of their heroes. Polynesians favored *maile*, a shrubby vine whose bark and leathery leaves give off a vanilla-like fragrance. It was used as a peace offering on the battlefield and was sacred to the *hula*.

First-time visitors often have a hard time appreciating *maile*. They would rather have their necks draped with orchids and plumeria instead of this plain-faced forest vine. But with enough patience they'll find that *maile* has a spirit and sensuality all its own. Its delicate, woodsy scent brings out the best in Hawai'i's perfumed flowers and lingers in the mind long after everything else has slipped away.

Maile, a member of the periwinkle family, grows throughout Hawai'i, although each island is known for its particular varieties. The *maile* on the Big Island tends to be large-leafed while that found on Oahu is more mid-sized. One of the most desired *lei* types is *maile laulii*, a round small-leafed *maile* gathered in the mountainous regions of Kauai.

To make a *maile lei* the leaves and bark are stripped free of the woody stem. The strands, usually three or more to a *lei*, are then twisted or knotted together and hung open-ended around the neck and shoulders. Sometimes the *maile* is intertwined with flowers such as *'ilima* or *pikake*.

Maile lei

Hawaiians associate the legendary *maile* with Laka, the goddess of the *hula*. It was placed on her altar and worn by the dancers. A *lei* worn in a hula was reserved for the goddess and never given away. Nathaniel B. Emerson recorded the following invocation to Laka in his 1909 book, *The Unwritten Literature of Hawaii, The Sacred Songs of the Hula:*

"O Laka ke akua pule ikaika,
Ua ku ka maile a Laka a imua,
Ua lu ka hua o ka maile..."

"The prayer to Laka has power,
The *maile* of Laka stands to the fore.
The *maile* vine casts now its seeds..."

Today, *maile lei* are worn at nearly every private and public occasion in Hawai'i, from birthdays and weddings to graduations. Afterwards they are taken home and draped over doorways, mantels, and picture frames. *Maile* is also used in Hawaii instead of ribbons at dedication ceremonies for everything from office buildings to hotels and gas stations. Scissors are left at home. During these Hawaiian blessings, the strands of *maile* are not cut but carefully untied.

Every Island Has Its *Lei*

The symbolic *lei* of Hawai'i's eight major islands blend togther in a symphony of color, fragrance, and texture. Some of these *lei* are made of flowers but others incorporate berries, leaves, stems, and seashells. While the links between the islands and their representative *lei* evolved naturally over time, in 1923 the Hawai'i Territorial Legislature officially adopted the concept of "*Na Lei o Hawai'i*."

O'AHU, *'ilima* (yellow-orange). *'Ilima lei* are sometimes called royal *lei* because they were once only worn by the high chiefs. The plants are abundant today but picking and stringing these *lei* is hard work. Hundreds of the paper-thin blossoms are required for a single strand.

HAWAI'I, *lehua* (red). The *'ohi'a lehua* tree grows on the volcanic slopes of the Big Island. Its pompom flower is sacred to Pele, the volcano goddess, and is often strung into a feathery, scarlet *lei*. While red is the most common color, its flowers may also be white, yellow, and orange.

MAUI, *lokelani* (pink). This small flower was not the first rose introduced to Hawai'i but it managed to survive the bite of the Japanese beetle. The *lokelani* or "rose of heaven" is usually mixed with ferns and other flowers.

KAUA'I, *mokihana* (purple). Found only on Kaua'i, this forest tree bears small seed capsules which smell like anise. The berries, which grow more fragrant as they dry, are strung like beads and several loops are needed for a *lei*. *Mokihana* is usually woven with strands of *maile*.

MOLOKA'I, *kukui* (silvery-green). The leaves and tiny white flowers of the *kukui* are braided together to make Moloka'i's *lei*. *Kukui* is nicknamed the candlenut because the oily kernels were once used in lamps and torches. Polished *kukui* nuts are also strung into *lei*.

LANA'I, *kaunaoa* (orange). This parasitic vine with inconspicuous flowers spreads out over low-lying plants. Its stringy orange stems are scooped up and gently twisted together to form a loosely-roped *lei*. *Kaunaoa*, which likes open wastelands, is called the "motherless plant."

KAHO'OLAWE, *hinahina* (silver-gray). *Hinahina*, a member of the Geranium family, grows on the sandy beaches of this island, just above the high water mark. The plant's hairy leaves give it a silvery appearance. The stems and flowering tips of the branches are braided together.

NI'IHAU, *pupu* (white). Hawai'i's most highly prized shell *lei* are made on Ni'ihau where the arid climate does not support all of the beautiful flowers found on the other islands. Shells of various color are gathered on the beaches, pierced, and strung on cords like pearls.

The Lei Maker

Theodore Wores, an artist who visited Honolulu a century ago, was particularly taken by the women who sat on the street corners making flower *lei*. He memorialized one of them in his famous 1901 painting, *The Lei Maker*, now in the collection of the Honolulu Academy of Arts. It depicts a young lady stringing a strand of delicate *'ilima* blossoms while seated on a *lauhala* frond mat.

Theodore Wores, *The Lei Maker*, 1901. Oil on canvas, 36 by 29 inches. Honolulu Academy of Arts. Gift of Drs. Ben and A. Jess Shenson.*Honolulu Academy of Arts*

Wores, the son of German-Hungarian immigrants, was born in San Francisco in 1859. His parents encouraged his early artistic talent and sent him abroad at the age of 16 to study at the Royal Academy in Munich. Upon completion of his studies he went to Italy, where he met the American expatriate artist James McNeill Whistler who was painting in Venice.

Inspired by Whistler's interest in Japanese art, Wores traveled to Japan in 1885 and became one of the first Western artists to depict scenes there of everyday life. On his way back to Japan in 1892, he stopped briefly in Hawai'i and returned for a longer stay in 1901. He painted *The Lei Maker* in a studio he rented on Beretania Street in downtown Honolulu.

During his long and adventurous career, Wores also painted in Samoa, England, Canada, New Mexico, and California. He died in 1939 in San Francisco and his work was not shown publicly again until the mid-1960s. His reputation was largely rescued by two San Francisco physicians, Ben and Jess Shenson, whose parents were good friends of the artist and his wife. They donated Wores' paintings to many museums and in 1986 gave *The Lei Maker* to the Honolulu Academy of Arts.

For many years the identity of Wores' model for *The Lei Maker* remained a mystery. She was finally identified through a photograph taken by the artist in his studio as Lizzie Victor, a Hawaiian who died in 1945 on the Big Island. It was rumored during her lifetime that Lizzie was fathered by King Kalakaua, a fact that might account for Wores posing her with an *'ilima* lei, a symbol of royalty.

Hawai'i's 1952 *Lei* Day queen and her attendants pose next to the Mission Memorial Building on King Street in Honolulu. *Bishop Museum*

Island beauties were always selected as the early May Day queens. After Hawai'i's recent cultural renaissance, mature women, schooled in the art of *lei* making and the Hawaiian language, became favored. *Bishop Museum*

First *Lei* Day Winners

The grand prize in Honolulu's first *Lei* Day contest on May 1, 1928 was worth $50. Earnest Parker picked up the check for an elaborate display of matching neck and hat *lei* made of orchids, marigolds, and daisies wrapped around a giant hat woven of *lauhala* fronds. Mrs. Peter Lee won the most beautiful *lei* award for her *kika*, or cigar flower *lei*, and Ellen Akana won the *lei* seller's award for her *lei* of violets, roses, baby's breath, and maiden hair fern.

Young *lei* sellers show off their creations at Kauluwela School *Lei* Day Celebration, 1948. *Bishop Museum*

May Day is *Lei* Day

A modern-day May Day court prepares to begin the festivities in Waikiki.

Lei Day, held every May first, is one of Hawai'i's most popular and colorful celebrations. Parades fill the streets, music fills the air, and anyone without a *lei* feels a bit undressed. The idea began in early 1928 when poet Don Blanding wrote a Honolulu newspaper article suggesting that a new holiday be created around the old island custom of making and wearing *lei*. Another writer, Grace Tower Warren, came up with the date May first and coined the phrase "May Day is *Lei* Day."

Honolulu's first *Lei* Day was held on May 1, 1928 and everyone in the city was encouraged to wear *lei*. Blanding made the rounds wearing five strands of *'ilima lei* and 11-strands of *mokihana*. Downtown festivities included Hawaiian music, *hula* dancing, flower exhibitions, strings of *maile* fluttering from maypoles, and *lei*-making contests. Nina Bowman, a vivacious 19-year-old University of Hawai'i student, was crowned the first *Lei* Day Queen on a throne of *ti* leaves.

The Honolulu *Star-Bulletin* reported on its front page that "lei blossomed on straw and felt hats, lei decorated automobiles, men and women and children wore them draped about their shoulders. To the city, Kamehameha's statue extended a garland of *maile* and plumeria, which fluttered in the wind from its extended hand. Lei recaptured the old spirit of the islands (a love of color and flowers, fragrance, laughter, and aloha."

Lei Day was made an official territorial holiday in 1929 and several years later the O'ahu ceremonies were moved to the courtyard of the Honolulu Hale (City Hall). Movie actress Dorothy Lamour made an appearance there in 1940 and presented that year's *Lei* Day Queen with a red carnation *lei* she had brought with her from California. World War II interrupted Hawai'i's normal *Lei* Day programs but by 1950 the festivities had returned with activities held at Honolulu Hale, the University of Hawai'i, and many local public and private schools.

Don Blanding, meanwhile, became well-known for his illustrated books of poetry such as *Vagabond's House*, *Let Us Dream*, *Drifter's Gold*, and a prose work, *Hula Moons*. He lived primarily in California but returned periodically to take part in the annual *Lei* Day events. Blanding's last book, *Hawaii Says Aloha*, was published in 1955. He died two years later and his ashes were scattered from *lei*-draped canoes off Waikiki Beach. Blanding's books are a staple in Hawai'i's second-hand bookstores.

Today's public *Lei* Day activities on O'ahu are centered at Kapi'olani Park in Waikiki, a practice that allows visitors to participate in the traditions of this popular holiday. Similar events are held on the Neighbor Islands. Buy a *lei* from the vendors or make one yourself. Wear it proudly for *Lei* Day is May Day in Hawai'i.

NOELANI

Today's May Day celebrations include exhibitions of Polynesian dance, a May Day court with princesses representing each of Hawai'i's major islands, vendor stands draped with fragrant offerings, a very competitive *lei* competition, and, of course, a May pole.

Boat Days

Prior to jet airline service, most Hawai'i visitors arrived and departed by ship. Boat Days were gala social events and the harbor docks were crowded with friends, tourism officials, hula girls, musicians, *lei* sellers, and news reporters looking for celebrities. It was a ritual for departing passengers to wait until their ships passed Diamond Head to throw a *lei* into the ocean. If it drifted back to shore they were assured of returning to the Islands.

Bishop Museum

Bishop Museum

First Kiss

The practice of presenting a *lei* with a kiss apparently began during World War II. According to one story a U.S.O. dancer took a shine to a Navy officer who was seated at a table in the audience. When the other entertainers dared her to give him a kiss she had the sudden inspiration to remove her *lei* and place it around his neck. She then gave him a kiss on the cheek and told him it was a Hawaiian custom. From that day forward it was.

Bishop Museum

Kamehameha Day

One of Hawai'i's favorite holidays is Kamehameha Day, June 11, celebrated the second weekend in June. It honors Kamehameha the Great, founder of the Hawaiian Kingdom. The main event in Honolulu is a Saturday parade that begins at Iolani Palace and passes through Waikiki. Each island sponsors a princess who rides a horse over the route decked out with leis representing that island. Kamehameha's statue across from Iolani Palace is also draped with long flower leis.

Bishop Museum

Sweet Potato *Lei*

Nursing mothers in Hawai'i used to wear *lei* of woven sweet potato vines which grew near the seashore. They would slap their chests with the *lei* to increase the flow of breast milk. Surfers also favored the *lei*. If they didn't like the size of the waves they would slap the water to make them bigger. Fishermen sometimes struck the water if they wanted to increase their catch.

New Year's *Lei*

Hala lei, made from the fruit of the pandanus tree, are found in various forms throughout Polynesia. According to a Hawaiian legend, the goddess Hiiaka was asked by a *kahuna* to save a terminally ill man while she was wearing a *hala lei*. She said she couldn't help because he was already dead. A *hala lei* is sometimes worn for good luck on New Year's Day to symbolize the passing of the old year and the arrival of the new.

Bishop Museum

Everywhere you Look

It's easy to buy a *lei* in Hawai'i. They are found in all flower shops and at stands located at the various airports, resort hotels, and tourists areas. Old-time Honolulu residents often head down to Maunakea Street which was lined with *lei* shops during World War II. Some of these shops are still in business today.

Bishop Museum

Blue Pheasant *Lei*

Hawai'i's *lei* makers use the feathers of many birds for their *lei* but one of the most prized is the pheasant. A blue pheasant *lei* is made from tiny fingernail-sized feathers that are plucked from the ring that encircles the neck. Since there is a limited amount of these ring feathers per bird, the average pheasant hat *lei* requires feathers from more than 100 birds.

Bishop Museum

Venus *Lei*

Hawai'i's *lei* makers created a special souvenir *lei* to commemorate the transit of Venus in 1874. They strung stiff, white paper that was cut and crumpled to represent the twinkling points of the bright planet. While the local people called these garlands *hoku* (star) *lei*, foreign visitors referred to them as "Venus *Lei*." These paper *lei* remained popular through the rest of the decade.

Princess of the Peacocks

Princess Kaiulani, once heir to the throne, grew up in the enchanted Waikiki estate of Ainahau. Peacocks roamed through gardens of her favorite *lei* flower, the fragrant white Arabian jasmine. When she died in 1899, at the age of 23, the cry of her peacocks could be heard for miles around. Kaiulani's jasmine is now known as *pikake*, the Hawaiian name for peacocks.

Baker-Van Dyke Collection

Old Gray Beard

Sanford B. Dole became the first and only president after the overthrow of the monarchy. When Spanish moss was introduced to the Islands during the 1920s the plant became popular in making *lei*. Clumps of Spanish moss reminded many Hawaiians of Dole's bushy gray beard and they called it *'umi 'umi* Dole or "Dole's Beard."

Ti Bags

There weren't any plastic bags or cardboard boxes in ancient Hawai'i. Perishable flower *lei* were often carried from place to place in *ti* leaf containers. A foot-long stalk of *ti* plant was cut and turned upside down on a flat surface. *Lei* were then piled on the stalk and the overlapping leaves were pulled up around the *lei* and tied.

Saintly Damien

Lei are often seen on the boxy statue of Father Damien that stands in front of the State Capitol Building facing Beretania St. Damien De Veuster, a young Sacred Heart priest from Belgium, came to Hawai'i in 1873 and volunteered to serve the leprosy colony at Kalaupapa on Molokai. He died of the disease himself in 1866. Today, the "Martyr of Molokai" is one of Hawai'i's most beloved heroes. If you have an extra *lei* nobody deserves it more than Damien.

Feather Flower

It takes hundreds of flowers and a lot of time to make an *'ilima lei*, the favored flower *lei* of the upper classes. One reason for its popularity is that the *'ilima* blossoms, when strung flat through the center, resemble the feather *lei* of ancient royalty. Unlike feather *lei*, however, the *'ilima lei* was a royal *lei* that could be worn by the common people.

Toxic *Lei*

Princess Ruth Keelikalani, described in 1874 as "the largest and richest woman in the islands," wasn't afraid of anything. Perhaps that's why she loved wearing *lei* of pink oleander, a member of the periwinkle family. Unless you have a similar strength of character leave those pretty oleander blossoms on the bush. The plant is so poisonous that even the insects stay away.

Paniolo Pansy

If you're sitting around a campfire on the Parker Ranch you might hear the story of Jack Purdy, the Big Island cattleman who planted the first pansies at Waimea in the early 1850s. These flowers thrived in the cool heights and he gave them the Hawaiian name of *pua po'o kanaka*, or "flower like a human face." The pansy became a symbol of the Hawaiian cowboys, (*paniolo*), on the Parker Ranch and are woven into *haku* hat and neck *lei*. The *lei* pictured is a similar species called *'ola'a* beauty.

Haku Lei

There is no such thing as a *haku* flower. The word "*haku*" refers to a traditional *lei* making technique in which blossoms, leaves, and fruits are braided or sewn face out into a background of greenery. Creating a *haku* allows *lei* makers to use non-traditional flowers and exercise the full powers of their creativity. Roses, pansies, and zinnias are popular *haku* flowers.

Lei Fashions

Lei, like clothing, go in and out of fashion. New flower combinations are introduced, *lei* makers try different styles, and celebrities popularize certain *lei*. To keep up with the trends visit the *Lei* Day *lei* contest gallery at Kapiolani Park in Honolulu or the hula performances at the annual Merrie Monarch Festival in Hilo, on the Big Island. Good ideas spread around the islands like wildfire.

Best of the *Lei*

The best of Hawai'i's *lei* makers wait for *Lei* Day (May first) to show off their stuff. If you're in Honolulu, head down to Kapiolani Park where the Department of Parks and Recreation sponsors an annual *lei* making contest that draws contestants from all of the islands. Awards are given to the top *lei* in a number of categories and the winners are displayed in an outdoor gallery. The *lei* makers also put on demonstrations for the public.

Ship Shape

Most flower *lei* may be worn or shipped from Hawai'i to the mainland. Some, however, are known to harbor insect pests. The restricted flowers include the island rose, gardenia, jade vine, *maunaloa*, and any plants in soil. Buy from a knowledgeable florist and let them airmail your gift *lei* back home for weddings and graduations.

Seaweed *Lei*

In the old days Hawaiians who lived near the seashore would go out at low tide and gather seaweed or *limu* off the reef. They braided the wet strands into *lei* and offered them to the gods associated with the ocean. Some seaweed *lei* were taken home and hung out in the sun to dry. These were later pounded into a powder that could be mixed with water and used as a medicated salve for bruises and wounds.

Lei Kitsch

Visitors only familiar with flower *lei* are in for a surprise if they attend Hawai'i high school carnivals or graduation ceremonies. Along with the flowers they'll see *lei* made with dollar bills, crack seeds, candy suckers, and Lifesavers. Other kitsch *lei* incorporate cigars and miniature whiskey bottles. Some island souvenir shops also sell plastic flower *lei* and false *'ilima lei* made of orange yarn.

Leid in Hawaii

Tourists love T-shirts with printed slogans. If you're young, frisky, and don't mind getting slapped, you can probably get away with "I Got Leid in Hawaii" or "I Wanna Lei You." Otherwise play it safe and pick something else like "I love Hawai'i." What reads funny in Waikiki might not get the same laughs back home.

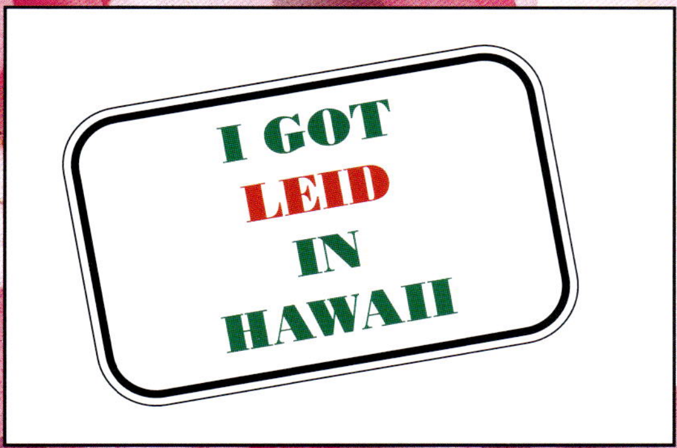

Lei on a Special Day

For special occasions the young in Hawai'i often buy *lei* for their dates instead of corsages. *Pikake* is especially popular at high school and college proms. The seriousness of the relationship used to be symbolized by the number of *pikake* strands the girl received. One or two strands represented a casual friendship while three or more indicated that romance was in flower. A wedding is the ultimate occasion where *lei* are worn making both bride a groom shine with *aloha*.

Lei Making Methods

Lei making is an art but it can be learned if you have time, patience, and a little bit of creativity in your fingertips. Don't worry if your first *lei* isn't quite what you expected. The great *lei* makers have been working their magic for years.

Start with an abundant supply of materials. A simple plumeria *lei* takes dozens of flowers while such favorites as *'ilima* and *kika lei* require thousands of blossoms. Flowers for these basic *lei* should be matched in color and size. If you are an adventurous *lei* maker you may want to experiment with various flowers and leaves in all sorts of combinations.

Ray Wong, a Hawai'i Kai *lei* maker who has won many *Lei* Day contest awards, told a local newspaper that "contrasting textures and color balance" distinguish prize-winning *lei*. "Once you've got the feel of a lei, the lei just flows," he said. "You can tell if a lei's good or not. If you don't feel the vibes, start again."

There are six basic ways to make a Hawaiian flower *lei*. The method used depends largely on tradition, suitability, and the individual style of the *lei* maker. Know your materials and practice good craftsmanship.

In ancient times the Hawaiians used tree and shrub fibers for string. They made their needles from the stiff mid-rib of a coconut leaf or thin stems of grass. Purists may still work that way but most modern *lei* makers use cotton thread and long steel needles that were introduced during the early 20th century.

While the basic *lei*-making methods have remained basically the same, new plant materials and floral combinations are always swinging in and out of favor. All it takes is a single *hula halau* strutting its stuff to launch a new *lei* making trend. Keep an eye out for surprises at the Merrie Monarch and other *hula* festivals and the annual *Lei* Day celebrations.

Lauhala baskets serve as flower receptacles for these two Hawaiian *lei* makers. *Bishop Museum*

Wili means to weave or wrap. Bougainvillea and other flowers and ferns are gently wrapped around a sturdy core (sometimes *ti* leaf, *lauhala*, or palm midribs, or pipe cleaners) to produce some of the most treasured *lei* in Hawai'i *Nei*.

Kui, or stringing method. The material is pierced through the center or side with a needle and held together by a single string. Plumeria, orchids, and carnations are popular stringing flowers.

Kipuu, or knotting method. Leafy vines or stems are knotted together to make a long-enough *lei* to drape around the neck and shoulders.

Hili, or braiding method. Strands of a single material are braided together. *Maile*, lacy ferns, and *ti* leaves are often braided together for *lei*.

Wili, or winding method. Materials are cut in short lengths and wound together. The center cord is often made of ferns, dried banana stalks, or ***ti*** leaves.

Humu-papa, or sewing method. Flowers and foliage are sewn onto a foundation. Banana and ***ti*** leaves are traditional background material.

Haku, or display method. Additional flowers, berries, and leaves are set, like fine jewels, into a background of foliage. Roses and chrysanthemums are often used in ***haku lei***.

Agnes Moka'iwi, one of Hawai'i's noteable *lei* sellers, offers her floral *lei* near Aloha Tower, Honolulu Harbor, 1941.

Lei sellers positioned themselves along the road to the old airport to attract both incoming and outgoing sales. Today the names on these signs grace the stalls at the new airport vendor stands.

Maunakea Street has a long history as the *lei* and floral center of downtown Honolulu.

Lei for Sale

Lei selling is not what it used to be. There are still old-timers around who remember the days before World War II when groups of Hawaiian women used to sit along the sidewalks of Maunakea Street, stringing and selling their *lei*. Out in Waikiki the *lei* sellers hung around the Moana, Royal Hawaiian, and Halekulani hotels or parked their junk cars along the curb and sold their wares from rolled-down windows.

Many *lei* sellers also headed down to Honolulu Harbor when the Matson liners came in or out of port. They wandered through the crowds with armfuls of *lei* as the hula girls danced, the streamers unfurled, and the Royal Hawaiian Band played favorite island tunes. Plump strands of carnations, plumeria, and ginger went for less than a quarter.

The newly renovated *lei* stands at the Honolulu International Airport.

By 1920 the introduction of long steel needles had turned *lei* making into a family affair. Mothers taught their daughters how to string plumeria and orchids before they started school. Most *lei* sellers before World War II grew flowers in their backyards or in neighborhood gardens. As times changed they began to rely on wholesalers who shipped in blooms from rural flower farms on Oahu and the Neighbor Islands.

When commercial jet service arrived at Honolulu International Airport in 1959, the *lei* sellers were already there. The first airport *lei* sellers sold their goods from the backs of trucks and established an order in line. When the airport built its first row of *lei* stands in 1952, it assigned them to the truck drivers in the same order. Most of the current *lei* stand operators are members of these original Hawaiian truck families. They lease the stands from the government and also pay a monthly percentage of their income.

An open-air *lei* shop on Maunakea Street in downtown Honolulu.

It's impossible to buy a *lei* for a quarter anymore but they're still a bargain when you consider how long it takes to pick and string the hundreds of flowers needed for some of Hawai'i's most popular *lei*. They also last longer thanks to the wonders of modern refrigeration. You can buy a *lei* today, cool it down tonight, and wear it again tomorrow.

All flowers, however, are not created equal. While orchids and carnations *lei* can be worn for two or three days, the fragile *pua kenikeni* begins to turn brown after a few hours. You can extend the life of plumeria and ginger by wrapping them in damp newspapers and storing them in the refrigerator vegetable bin. Others, such as *pikake* and tuberose, will last longer if they are kept cool and dry in a produce bag. Ask your *lei* seller for advice.

BLUE PHEASANT *LEI*

Hawai'i's *lei* makers use the feathers of many birds for their *lei* but one of the most prized is the pheasant. A blue pheasant *lei* is made from tiny fingernail-sized feathers that are plucked from the ring that encircles the neck. Since there is a limited amount of these ring feathers per bird, the average pheasant hat *lei* requires feathers from more than 100 birds.

Feather Lei

The ancient Hawaiians, who dwelled in forests full of colorful native birds, reached their highest level of artistry in featherwork. Captain Cook collected dozens of feather capes, cloaks, helmets, *lei*, and ceremonial items on his voyages. He believed that the beauty, design, and craftsmanship of these velvety objects were a match for anything then produced in Europe.

One of the most unusual Hawaiian feather objects was the *kahili*, a wooden pole topped by a cylinder usually made of seabird feathers. These kahili were used as standards and protective agents for individuals of high rank. They were waved over the heads of royalty and carried in funeral processions to ward off evil spirits.

Most of the garment and *lei* feathers came from birds that are now either extinct or endangered. They were captured in the forests by professionals bird catchers who studied the behavior of each species and devised traps and nets to snare them. Demand for their skills was high since thousands of feathers were needed for each garment or *lei*. The feathers were usually attached to coconut husk with thread from the banana plant.

Pheasant and peacock feather hat bands are prized for their artistic design, construction, and color.

The rarest feather color in Hawai'i was yellow and it became a symbol of royalty. Yellow feathers came from two beautiful forest birds, the *'o'o* and *mamo*. Both were predominantly black with small tufts of yellow feathers around the wings and tail. These birds were caught and let go after their tufts were removed. Red feathers were provided by the *i'iwi* and *'apapane*, and green feathers from the *'o'u*.

While feather capes, cloaks, and helmets were reserved for male chiefs, royal women were allowed to wear feather *lei* (*lei hulu*). These ornamental *lei* were worn atop the head, around the neck, or hung untied down from the shoulders. *Lei* of a single color, especially yellow, were more prized than *lei* of mixed colors. They are still passed down through Hawaiian families as treasured heirlooms.

Hawaiian featherwork expert John Dominis Holt wrote that he learned the value of feather *lei* to his people when he was growing up. "People who made them, who wore them, who had strong feelings as my grandmother did, thought in terms of giving them love. When she aired them she would run her hands down the length of a lei. She would say things in Hawaiian as if she were talking to children."

Today's rounded feather *lei* are tied or sewn to a central cotton or silk cord while the feathers for flat-back *lei*, popular for hatbands, are usually sewn to a band of felt. Pheasant and peacock feathers are now used for hatbands and chicken feathers are dyed yellow and red to represent the royal *lei* of the past. Feather *lei* making takes time, patience, and concentration. The most beautiful examples are a bargain at any price.

***Keiki* dress in costume and head *lei* for a school May Day program.**

At the end of each sport season, seniors of the University of Hawai'i receive mounds of *lei* to honor their achievements.

***Tutu* drape themselves with the regal elegance of flower *lei*.**

Graduation, a landmark event in any child's life, is commemorated with *lei* of seed, flower, shell, candy, and a new tradition: money.

Royal Respect

During ancient times the hands of commoners were never allowed to rise above the head of their chiefs. If you were given permission to present a *lei* to a member of the royal class (*ali'i*) it was delivered with a respectful bow or handed to an attendant. Some *lei* which were especially difficult to make, or included rare flowers or feathers, were reserved for the highest ranking chiefs.

Lei Etiquette

'Ohai-ali'i Lei

There are no hard and fast rules about wearing *lei* in Hawai'i. You can wear any kind of *lei*, anytime and for any occasion. It's even okay to wear a *lei* for no other reason than to celebrate being here and to add a touch of *aloha* to your day.

About the only thing you don't want to do is refuse a *lei* that someone gives you. This is not the time to be shy. Welcome the *lei* with a big smile, a hug, and a little peck on the cheek. This is why you came to Hawai'i.

Some people, of course, are sensitive to island flowers and scents. If you are bothered by a fragrant *lei* wait for a lull in the conversation and slip it off unobtrusively. If you're smothered with *lei* at a commencement or farewell party, take a break and drape the heaviest over your arm. Or give a few away. Nobody expects you to wear dozens of *lei* piled up to your eyeballs.

The reverse also makes sense. If you think that someone might be allergic to fragrances ask the florist for an unscented *lei*. Watch out, too, for women wearing delicate white fabrics that might pick up flower stains. If you're giving a *lei* to someone from an unfamiliar culture make sure that body contact among strangers is not considered impolite. And if you do lean in to give a kiss watch out that you don't get too close. Fleshy flowers such as *pua kenikeni* are easily bruised.

Old-timers will tell you that certain *lei* are only good for men or women. The *kika* or cigar flower *lei*, for example, is often called a "man's *lei*" while the frilly *'ohai-ali'i lei* is often called a "woman's *lei*." Don't fret over the distinction. Most of the *lei* you buy at the *lei* stands or in the flower shops are perfectly suited for either sex.

There are, however, some taboos. Don't give a *lei* to a pregnant woman. Some consider this bad luck for the unborn child. And don't put a *hala lei* around the neck of a politician. This beautiful fruit of the *hala* tree is supposed to represent the coming of the end and a time to move on to new things. It's a good *lei* for New Year's fun but not for someone on the campaign trail. You wouldn't want to be responsible for his or her not getting elected.

Common Lei Flowers

Bougainvillea
Bougainvillea spectablis

Bougainvilleas, native to South America, have been grown in Hawai'i since the early 19th century. The papery bracts come in many colors, from bright orange and red to deep purple. A single *lei* consists of hundreds of flowers strung through the center or attached in bunches. The fiery bougainvillea is sometimes called *pua kepalo* or devil's flower.

Carnation
Dianthus caryophyllus

The Protestant missionaries brought the carnation from New England during the mid-1800s and fields of carnations were once a common sight along island roads. Some flower farms still grow carnations today but it is now just as economical to import these long-lasting flowers. Red carnation *lei* are usually worn by men and white carnation *lei* by women.

◄ Cigar Flower
Cuphea ignea

These half-inch flowers, plucked from short shrubs, have white or orange-red tubes. Introduced in the late-1800s, the Hawaiians thought they resembled a tiny lit cigar. Hundreds of blossoms are strung laterally between the base and mouth, in various bead-like patterns, to make this *lei*. It is often given to men because of the color and cigar connotation.

Coronation Flower

King Kalakaua, the first Hawaiian monarch to have a European-style coronation, loved carnations. His subjects got the two confused and called the flower *poni mo'i*, their word for coronation. George Ariyoshi, Hawai'i's governor for much of the 1980s, wore red carnation *lei* to all state events. It became known as the Ariyoshi *lei*.

Crownflower
Calotropis gigantea

The crownflower is a lavender or pale greenish-white flower with a subtle scent. It was a favorite of Queen Liliuokalani because its five petals surrounding a solid center resemble a royal crown. The whole flower is usually strung lengthwise but sometimes the petals are removed and the crowns bumped together. The milky sap can irritate the skin and eyes.

Gardenia
Gardenia augusta

The white gardenia was introduced from China and its fragrant scent is said to arouse sexual feelings. *Lei* makers remove the calyx and lower portion of the flower tube and string the flowers lengthwise. The tiare (Gardenia taitensis) is a small gardenia native to the Society Islands and is a favorite *lei* flower of Tahitians living in Hawai'i.

'Ilima
Sidex fallax

The *'ilima* was probably the only plant that was cultivated by the early Hawaiians specifically for *lei* making. Even today there are *lei* makers who specialize in *'ilima* and turn their back yards over to these bushes. The papery, golden-orange flowers have five petals and are an inch in diameter. The blossoms are strung through the center.

◄ Maunaloa
Canavalia cathartica

This pea blossom vine has white and lavender blossoms which are picked unopened and strung through the calyx. The wing and keel petals are alternated and the top petal is bent back to lay flat. *Maunaloa lei* cannot be taken to the Mainland due to an insect that infests the flower. For this reason a substitute *maunaloa*-style *lei* is made with purple vanda orchids.

CROWN OF *LEI*

Lavender crown flowers, native to China and India, were brought to Hawai'i in the late 1800s. They were a favorite of Queen Liliuokalani, the last of the Hawaiian monarchs. Crown flower *lei* became especially popular after her death in 1917. The white crown flower was introduced around 1920 and during World War II, imitation crown flower *lei* were carved from ivory and sold in island jewelry shops.

'Ohi'a Lehua

Metrosideros polymorpheaa

The *'ohi'a lehua*, native to Hawai'i's dry forests, grows at a high elevation and thrives near new volcanic lava flows. Its most common flower color is red but there are also yellow and white varieties. *Lei* are made by tying clusters of flowers by their stems to a central cord. Because of the hardness of the tree, its pompom blossoms symbolize stability and strength.

Pakalana

Telosma Cordata

This slender little vine boasts yellow-green, trumpet-shaped flowers about a half-inch in diameter. Their lemon-like fragrance is unusual but quite pleasant. *Pakalana* blossoms are strung lengthwise or through their sides. It takes about 150 flowers to make a single strand but most *pakalana lei* include several strands.

RAIN MAKER

The red flowers of the *'ohi'a lehua* tree are sacred to Pele, the volcano goddess. In ancient times *lei* made from the blossoms were offered to Pele and thrown into the crater at Kilauea on the Big Island. The *lei* were fashioned on the spot because it was believed that picking a *lehua* on the way up the mountain would bring rain.

Pikake

Jasminum Sambac

The Chinese brought this Arabian jasmine to Hawai'i but the Hawaiians claimed it as their own. A favorite of Princess Kaiulani, they named it *"pikake"* after the peacocks who roamed through her gardens near Waikiki. *Lei* strung with this fragrant white flower, a familiar part of the courtship ritual, are believed to be a sure way to a woman's heart.

Plumeria

Plumeria acuminata, rubra, obtusa

Plumeria trees were introduced to Hawai'i in the mid-1800s. They are easy to maintain and produce long-lasting, fragrant flowers. While the first local plumeria were yellow, today's varieties include white, pink, and red in a variety of combinations. Today the plumeria, usually strung lengthwise through its center, is Hawai'i's most popular *lei* flower.

Pua Kenikeni
Fagraea berteirana

Pua kenikeni trees, introduced to Hawai'i in the late 1800s from the South Pacific, were first cultivated in windward Oahu. The fragrant tubular flowers bloom white and then turn to yellow and orange. They are strung lengthwise and are highly perishable. At one time these flowers sold for 10 cents each and the Hawaiian name, "*pua kenikeni*," means "dime flower."

Stephanotis
Stephanotis Floribunda

The Hawaiian name for the fragrant stephanotis is *pua male*, the marriage flower, because it is a traditional favorite for bridal *lei* and wedding bouquets. The waxy white, five-petal flowers belong to the milkweed family and are native to Madagascar. For *lei* the flowers are strung lengthwise through their trumpet-shaped tubes.

Tuberose
Polianthes tuberosa

A fragrant herb of the amaryllis family, the tuberose is a native of Mexico. Its bulbous flowers are usually strung lengthwise through their centers and sometimes combined with other flowers such as carnations. The tuberose, a great favorite of visitors, is also popular with *lei* makers because it is usually abundant throughout the year.

Tahitian Treat

Kenneth P. Emory, the great Pacific anthropologist, had a trademark flower *lei*. On his first trip to Tahiti in 1925 he found a wife and, as a wedding present, received two *pua kenikeni* trees which he planted in his yard back in Honolulu. Emory strung the fragrant golden-orange flowers into *lei* every morning and presented them to his co-workers at the Bishop Museum. In 1983 the museum dedicated a grove of *pua kenikeni* in his honor.

Vanda orchid
Vanda hookeriana x V. teres

The vanda orchid was developed in Singapore during the 1890s and became widely known after Hawai'i growers began mass marketing it to the mainland after World War II. Vandas are relatively long-lasting and come in a range of colors. Basic "single" *lei* are made by stringing the flowers, petals intact, through the center.